I WANT TO KNOW

Are Monsters Real?

Portia Summers and
Dana Meachen Rau

Enslow Publishing
101 W. 23rd Street
Suite 240
New York, NY 10011
USA
enslow.com

Published in 2017 by Enslow Publishing, LLC
101 W. 23rd St., Suite 240, New York, NY 10011

Library of Congress Cataloging-in-Publication Data

Names: Summers, Portia, author.
Title: Are monsters real? / Portia Summers and Dana Meachen Rau.
Description: New York : Enslow Publishing, 2017. | Series: I want to know |
  Includes bibliographical references and index.
Identifiers: LCCN 2016024760| ISBN 9780766082465 (library bound) | ISBN
  9780766082441 (pbk.) | ISBN 9780766082458 (6-pack)
Subjects: LCSH: Monsters—Juvenile literature.
Classification: LCC GR825 .S86 2016 | DDC 001.944—dc23
LC record available at https://lccn.loc.gov/2016024760

Printed in China

To Our Readers: We have done our best to make sure all websites in this book were active and appropriate when we went to press. However, the author and the publisher have no control over and assume no liability for the material available on those websites or on any websites they may link to. Any comments or suggestions can be sent by email to customerservice@enslow.com.

Photo Credits: Cover Michael Rosskothen/Shutterstock.com; pp. 3, 13 Vuk Kostic/Shutterstock.com; p. 5 © iStockphoto.com/vukkostic; p. 7 Doug Gray/Illustration Works/Getty Images; p. 8 iStockphoto.com/Marc Dufresne; p. 11 David De Lossy/Digital Vision/Getty Images; p. 14 Yuri Cortez/AFP/Getty Images; p. 15 Paul Biris/Moment/Getty Images; p. 16 Stefano Bianchetti/Corbis Historical/Getty Images; p. 17 Silver Screen Collection/Moviepix/Getty Images; p. 19 © iStockphoto.com/ tinusbez; p. 20 The Asahi Shimbun/Getty Images; p. 21 Keystone/Hulton Archive/Getty Images; p. 22 Alan Smillie/Shutterstock.com; p. 24 Bettmann/Getty Images; p. 25 Andrew Rich/Vetta/Getty Images; p. 26 Forrest Anderson/The LIFE Images Collection/Getty Images; p. 27 Topical Press Agency/Hulton Archive/Getty Images.

Contents

Chapter 1

· · · · · · · · · · ·

Many Types of Monsters

When you imagine a monster, what do you see? A hairy beast with big claws and teeth? A three-headed reptile with glowing red eyes? A tall, pale creature with wings and webbed fingers? Where would you find such a thing? In a castle or a cave? In the swamp or in the sea? In the forest… or in your closet?

Monsters Around the World

Many people all over the world have been telling scary stories about monsters. Most of these monsters are huge, dangerous, and ugly. In Malaysia, the manticore stalks the forests; a creature with the body of a lion, the face of a man, and a mouth full of razor-sharp teeth, waiting for

Giants were known to be huge, strong, and bloodthirsty. Other stories tell of giants that kept treasure and were clumsy.

a chance to use it's snake-like tail tipped with poisoned darts against its victim. In the Alps, the heavy steps of giants make the ground shake. In North America, the wendigo [wen-DEH-go], a creature with long claws and a hunger for human flesh seeks out its next meal. In India, *rakshasas* [RAK-sha-sas] change into colorful animals, like tigers, bears, or monkeys. In the rainforests of the African Congo, the *mokèlé-mbèmbé* [MO-KAY-le UM-bam-bee] hides in caves along the riverbank and overturns canoes.

Monsters and Heroes

In many myths, heroes had to fight monsters. The Minotaur [MIN-uh-tawr] lived in an underground maze. He had a human body and a bull's head. The hydra [HI-druh] was a swamp creature with many heads. When one was cut off, two grew in its place. Cerberus [SUR-buh-rus] was a

Imagine That!

The most famous Gorgon was called Medusa. The famous Greek hero Jason faced her. When Medusa looked at her reflection in Jason's shiny shield, she turned herself into stone.

Frankenstein's monster is perhaps one of the most famous monsters in the world. According to the story by Mary Shelley, Dr. Victor Frankenstein stitched together body parts from **corpses** and brought his creation to life. The monster, called Adam, after the first man, terrified villagers and was eventually killed by an angry crowd.

Alone at night in your room, you hear a strange sound. A scratch against the floor, then a thump. Is it just a mouse? Your family pet? Or something far worse?

three-headed dog with sharp fangs and deadly drool. Gorgons were scaly witch-like creatures with snakes for hair that could turn a man to stone. Harpies were great flying beasts with the talons and body of a bird, but the face of a woman.

Why do people believe such wild tales? The dark of night is mysterious and can be scary. People can get carried away and imagine something threatening just around the next turn in the road, or underneath the bed. Even if you don't believe, are you still willing to get out of bed and check for yourself? Or does that strange noise sound just a little too spooky?

Chapter 2

Monsters of the Night

Before the days of large cities, many people lived in small **rural** villages. Villagers farmed their own crops. They depended on each other to survive. They were often scared of what might happen to their neighbors and their livestock. All across the world, these villagers imagined horrible creatures that lived in the nearby forests and mountains.

Lycanthropes

One such creature was the **lycanthrope** [LI-can-throw-p]. Werewolves are the most common type of lycanthrope. A werewolf was human during the day. At night, when

In the dark of night, a thick forest can be even scarier. Add some fog and some strange sounds, and it's easy to believe that something is lurking just behind the next tree.

the moon was full, it would grow hair, claws, and fangs. Then it would tear through villages, killing animals and people.

The werewolf legend developed all over the world. According to Greek tradition, Zeus punished King Lycaon by turning him and his children into wolves. Norse mythology says that the giant wolf Fenrir was bound by the gods in order for the world to keep turning. In France, the werewolf is called the *loup garou*. While the stories are more common in places with thicker forests, werewolf legends occurred in Italy and Portugal, as well.

Many werewolf stories say that a person may become a werewolf if they are bitten by a wolf. Others say that in order to become a werewolf, a person must be cursed by a **Gypsy**. Another common story told was that a person who drank rainwater from the footprint of a werewolf would become one on the next full moon.

It was true that there were wolves in forests, and a pack might attack villagers if they were hungry. And

Imagine
That

In Asia, where wolves don't live, there are few native werewolf stories. Instead, it is common to hear stories about weretigers. In Africa, the creatures are werehyenas.

There are many stories of terrifying werewolves who destroy villages, livestock, and even the brave warriors who try to defeat them.

some people may have suffered from a condition called **hypertrichosis** [HI-per-tre-KO-sis], which causes extra hair to grow on a person's body. Clinical lycanthropy is a mental condition in which a person imagines he or she is a wolf.

Hypertrichosis is very rare, but it can still be found today. Before the condition was understood by science, many people with hypertrichosis were thought to be werewolves.

Vampires

Another common monster in stories is the vampire. A vampire is someone who has already died, but rises from his or her coffin at night to drink the blood of other people. Like the werewolf, stories of this creature come from many places. The oldest vampire stories come from Babylonia over 6,000 years ago. But stories about vampires have been told in China, the Philippines, North America, UK, and, of course, Northern Europe. The most famous vampire story takes place in Transylvania (modern-day Romania).

This castle in Romania is known as Dracula's castle. It is thought to have inspired novelist Bram Stoker when he was writing about the famous Dracula.

The most famous vampire in the world, by far, is Count Dracula. Written in 1897 by Bram Stoker, *Dracula* told the story of an **undead** count who feeds off the blood of his visitors. It seems pretty unbelievable, but Stoker actually based his character off a real person from history. Vlad Dracul, also known as Vlad the Impaler was a prince in Walachia (Transylvania) during the mid-fifteenth century. He was known for being very cruel, and many rival rulers tried to kill him. However, the circumstances of his death aren't certain. And to this day, no one knows where he is buried, which is unusual for a prince.

Frightened villagers fought off vampires with garlic, bells, crosses, and lights. They dug up graves to find and destroy vampires. It was said that vampires could only come out at night, couldn't go into churches, and had red cheeks, long fingernails, and fangs.

Stories about vampires may have been told to explain death. **Infectious** disease sometimes killed many people at a time. The villagers did not understand how illnesses spread. They blamed people they thought were vampires. By destroying a vampire, they thought they could end the deaths.

Vampires were said to drink the blood of the living. They were known for being good-looking and charming, and even for having the power to control other people's minds when they needed. It was also said they could turn into bats and climb walls!

Chapter 3

· · · · · · · · · · ·

Monsters of the Sea

Throughout history, people have also feared monsters that come from seas and lakes. Sailors and fishermen described some of them as long snakes. Some had flippers and fins like a fish, or legs like a lizard. Vikings told stories of the Kraken. The Kraken had long, slimy **tentacles**. Its body was more than a mile wide. From a distance, sailors thought the Kraken was an island. But if they sailed too close, the Kraken would pull their ship underwater. Japanese sailors told stories of the kappa; which looked like a turtle, except for his human face. It would drown anyone who got too close to the water. **Aboriginal** Australians told stories of the bunyip, a type

Are the dark, murky waters of deep oceans and lakes home to terrible monsters? Some people think so.

of swamp monster with the head of an emu, the tail of a fish, and human feet that were turned backward. They would knock over boats and eat the fishermen inside.

Real-Life Sea Monsters

Did sailors really see monsters? Some water animals can look unusual. Maybe sailors really saw seals, crocodiles,

An oarfish is a sea creature that may have inspired the legend of the sea serpent. An oarfish can grow up to 36 feet (11 meters) long!

octopuses, turtles, sharks, or whales. The oarfish is an especially ugly fish that looks a lot like a monster.

Scientists think they have solved the mystery of the Kraken. Some of them thought the Kraken and other similar sea monsters might be colossal squid. No one could ever find one alive, however. Then in 2004, Japanese scientists finally saw this real "monster." The giant squid has a beak to tear its **prey**, and eight arms for grabbing. The average colossal squid is between 39 and 46 feet (12 to 14 meters) long!

The Loch Ness Monster

All over the world, communities tell lake monster stories. Canada has two famous ones. Champ lives in Lake Champlain. Ogopogo [oh-goh-POH-goh] lives in the Okanagan [oh-ka-NAgan] Lake that borders Quebec, Vermont, and New York.

Probably the most infamous lake monster in the world is "Nessie," the Loch Ness Monster. People have claimed to see this creature in Loch Ness, in Scotland, for almost 1,500 years. Witnesses describe her humped back, flippers, long tail, and long neck. Tourists still flock to Loch Ness to try to see her.

Imagine That!

The Lakota, Dakota, Cheyenne, Sioux, Kiowa, and many other American Indian tribes tell legends of the Unktehila (OOnk-tay-HEE-lah); a large, horned water serpent with massive jaws and teeth. These creatures were supposed to be responsible for many unexplained disappearances and deaths. Bones of these creatures (now known to be from dinosaurs) are still considered sacred to many tribes.

Other than Ogopogo and Champ, there are many other lake monsters in the United States. The Alkali Lake Monster of Nebraska has a smell as terrible as death itself. The Eel Pig of Herrington Lake in Kentucky likes to attack fishing boats. The Giant Octopus of Lake Thunderbird in Oklahoma is blamed for nearly every strange drowning in the lake. The Honey Island Swamp Monster of Louisiana has a different name and origin, depending on who you ask. However, one thing can be agreed on: this is no normal swamp animal.

Some people say Nessie is a **plesiosaur**. A plesiosaur is a type of marine dinosaur that supposedly went extinct 66 million years ago. They think plesiosaurs have somehow survived in Loch Ness. It is more likely that witnesses have seen large waves or giant fish, such as sturgeon or catfish. But people still keep looking. Scientists have even used special underwater submarines and **sonar** to look for her.

Chapter 4

· · · · · · · · · · ·

Curious Cryptids

A **cryptid** is an animal whose existence has been suggested, but never proved. Cryptids can live in oceans, forests, or mountains. Anywhere that is out of the way of humans is where cryptids can supposedly live. Chupacabra (CHOO-pa-KAH-brah; which means "goat sucker" in Spanish) is a creature that supposedly lives Latin America, and survives by drinking the blood from livestock. It is supposedly the size of a large dog, with reptilian skin, glowing eyes, and a row of spikes from its neck down the length of its back. In parts of the British Isles, a massive black **canine** with red eyes supposedly wanders the foggy hillsides looking for souls. In the

Pine Barrens of New Jersey, a flying **bipedal** horse with claws has stalked the woods since colonial times, killing livestock and anyone unfortunate enough to meet it face-to-face.

Crptids are some of the most famous legends in the world. The Jersey Devil, Bigfoot, and Mothman are all examples of this type of monster. George M. Eberhart of the American Library Association said: "Cryptids must be big, weird, dangerous, or significant to humans in some way."

Bigfoot

Perhaps the most famous cryptid in the America is Bigfoot. Bigfoot may roam the woods of the Pacific North West. Thousands of folks have claimed they saw footprints, hair, or even Bigfoot himself. They say he is a huge ape-like creature covered with brown and black hair. Even American Indians saw him long ago. They called him Sasquatch. Skeptics think that the hair and footprints are from bears.

Imagine That!

Another famous cryptid is the Mongolian Death Worm, who supposedly lives in the Gobi Desert. Witnesses claim the creature is a fat, red worm about 4 ft (1 m) long. It supposedly produces poison from its skin and a jolt of electricity powerful enough to kill a camel.

Gigantopithecus

Like Nessie, there might be an ancient answer to the Bigfoot mystery. Gigantopithecus (ji-gan-to-PITH-a-kuss) was an ape that existed up until about one hundred thousand years ago in Asia. The creature is a distant relative to the modern orangutan, and stood up to ten feet (3 meters) tall and weighed up to 595 pounds (270 kilograms)!

In the Himalaya Mountains, this creature is called the Yeti. Villagers tell stories of the yeti, or Abominable Snowman, coming down from the mountains to attack villages. In the Australian wilderness, this creature is called the Yowie. In India and Bangladesh, it is called the Mande Barung.

Many fans and believers have attempted to collect proof of these creatures' existence. They have studied footprints in the snow and "yeti skins" kept by villagers. Scientists decided the skins were from bears or yaks. So were the tracks. As snow melts, it makes tracks look larger than their original size. Believers say there are still many unexplored parts of the forest and the mountains. They think huge, hairy creatures could live there.

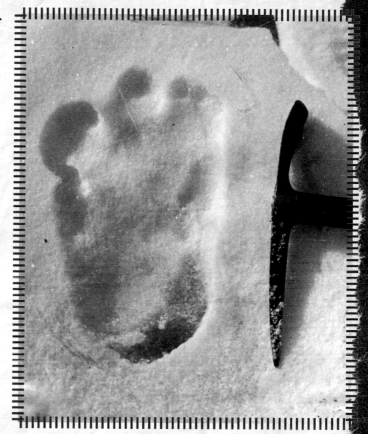

Mentioning Monsters

Today, books and movies tell monster stories. We tell spooky tales around campfires. The dark can be scary. Strange things happen. People have seen furry giants in the woods across the world for hundreds of years. Others hear unexplained noises, or see massive creatures swimming in lakes. What could they be? Could they be monsters?

Words to Know

Aboriginal The native peoples of Australia.

bipedal Walking upright on two legs.

canine A dog.

corpse A dead body.

cryptid An animal whose existence is suggested, but not proved.

extinct A species that is no longer living.

Gypsy A travelling race of people who traditionally live in Europe and speak Romany. They are known for telling fortunes and cursing and blessing people who they believe deserve it.

hypertrichosis [HI-per-tree-koh-sis] A disease which causes extra hair to grow all over their body.

infectious Likely to be caught by other people.

lycanthrope a person who can change form during the full moon, specifically into that of a wolf.

marine Having to do with the water; specifically living in it.

myth A story told to explain the past or describe unbelievable creatures.

plesiosaur A swimming dinosaur with a long neck and limbs that helped it paddle through water.

rural An area where not many people live.

sonar A tool scientists use to find something underwater.

tentacles The long limbs of some sea animals that are used to grab, feel, and move through the water.

Further Reading

Books

Animal Planet. *Finding Bigfoot: Everything You Need to Know.* New York, NY: Feiwel & Friends Publishing, 2013.

McCall, Gerrie and Chris McNab. *Mythical Monsters Legendary, Fearsome Creatures.* New York, NY: Scholastic, 2011.

Redfern, Nick. *The Bigfoot Book: The Enyclopedia of Sasquatch, Yeti and Cryptid Primates.* Canton, MI: Visable Ink Press, 2015.

Wright, John D. *Cryptids and Other Creepy Creatures: The World of Unsolved Mysteries.* New York, NY: Scholastic, 2009.

Websites

How Stuff Works

*animals.howstuffworks.com/animal-facts/
    cryptozoology.htm*

Read more about more cryptids.

International Cryptozoology Museum

cryptozoologymuseum.com

Visit the site of the International Cryptozoology Museum
in Portland, Maine.

KidzWorld

*www.kidzworld.com/article/24861-the-legend-of-
vampires*

Learn more facts about vampires.

Index